Hometown Hospitals: The Weakest Link? Bioterrorism Readiness in America's Rural Hospitals

Elin A. Gursky, Sc.D.
Senior Fellow for Biodefense and Public Health
ANSER Institute for Homeland Security

Report Commissioned by the National Defense University

Center for Technology and National Security Policy

June 2004

Contents

Acknowledgements

The author extends deep appreciation and gratitude to the participants of this study, without whose interest, time, and assistance this report would not have been possible. Five hospital chief executive officers, their medical and nursing staff and managerial personnel, and representatives from each hospital's community, including elected officials and emergency responders, provided candid and critical insights that helped frame key areas of concern regarding rural hospital preparedness.

The author also gratefully acknowledges the experts who served as reviewers for this report. Their critical assessments contributed to the report's quality and its potential to impact preparedness efforts in the hospital and clinical communities. These experts are as follows:

James D. Bentley, Ph.D., American Hospital Association

Teresa Brown, MSW, MPH, Health Resources and Services Administration

Paul A. Castillo, M.D., MPH, Chemical/Bioterrorism Preparedness Consultant

Frank E. Ferrante, Johns Hopkins University

Roger L. Harrell, MHA, Dorchester County Health Department, Maryland

Linda O'Brien, RN, BSN, CIC, Doctor's Hospital, Maryland

Cheryl Peterson, RN, MSN, American Nurses Association

Richard A. Raymond, M.D., Nebraska Health and Human Services System

Mark S. Smith, M.D., Washington Hospital Center, DC

Colonel Donald F. Thompson, M.D., MPH & TM, U.S. Northern Command

Many thanks to Patrick Sullivan, research intern at the ANSER Institute for Homeland Security, for his tireless support of all phases of this project. Thanks also to Neil Vibhakar, research intern at the ANSER Institute for Homeland Security, for his assistance and support in scheduling and coordinating meetings at participating hospitals, and to Colleen Laughlin, research assistant at the ANSER Institute for Homeland Security, for arranging travel to the hospital sites.

Finally, the author commends the Center for Technology and National Security Policy of the National Defense University for commissioning this study and its concern for the bioterrorism preparedness efforts of rural hospitals and their role in homeland security.

Elin A. Gursky, Sc.D.
Senior Fellow for Biodefense and Public Health
The ANSER Institute for Homeland Security

Executive Summary

Over the past decade, acts of international and domestic terrorism have demonstrated to government officials and policy makers the urgency of preparing systems to support the detection of atypical health events and the provision of preventive and interventional medical services in mass-care events. The 1995 bombing of the Alfred P. Murrah Federal Building in Oklahoma City resulted in 168 deaths and required the efforts of nearly 5,500 emergency responders dispatched to the scene over 17 days in chaotic and feverish attempts to rescue and facilitate subsequent medical and surgical interventions to save the lives of over 600 injured victims.[1] The September 11, 2001, attacks on the World Trade Center and the Pentagon resulted in over 3,000 deaths and nearly 2,400 injured.[2] The lethality of the attacks averted strain on hospitals but, once again, required the coordinated efforts of emergency responders and medical providers. The anthrax attacks of 2001 resulted in relatively few victims. However, despite 22 illnesses, including five deaths,[3] hospitals in the five anthrax epicenters were required to institute triage for a novel disease and to devise new protocols of health screening, prophylaxis, and treatment. Eventually both public health and medical care systems were required to dispense antibiotics to an estimated 32,000 individuals.[4] On March 11, 2004, terrorist bombings on several trains in Madrid resulted in nearly 200 deaths and about 1,800 injured.[5] Madrid's hospitals were swamped with casualties as the hospitals appealed urgently for blood donations.[6]

Acts of terrorism upon civilian populations necessitate a robust response by health and medical care systems and present particular challenges to the United States' almost 5,000 acute care hospitals. As the locus of medical diagnosis and intervention for a wide array of routine activities ranging from the provision of primary care for the uninsured to the delivery of tertiary procedures for life-threatening diseases, hospitals face the quandary of terrorism preparedness and response with limited budgets and insufficient numbers of trained human resources. These needs are even more acutely experienced by the nation's approximately 2,000 rural hospitals, which have a comparatively smaller repertoire of medical resources yet face unique vulnerabilities.

The spectrum of weapons of mass destruction demands a diverse set of response capabilities. The use of an explosive device necessitates an urgent and massive medical effort to save the lives of injured persons not immediately killed. Conversely, the deployment of a biological agent in most instances unleashes a communicable pathogen, the required response to which grows greater over time as the incidence of human infection increases. The resulting epidemic is workforce consuming, requiring voluminous

---

[1] Final Report of the American Psychological Association Task Force on the Mental Health Response to the Oklahoma City Bombing, July 1997.

[2] September 11 News Online; statistics current as of 2002 and compiled from CNN and Reuters; http://www.september11news.com.

[3] Elin Gursky, Thomas V. Inglesby, and Tara O'Toole, "Anthrax 2001: Observations on the Medical and Public Health Response," *Biosecurity and Bioterrorism: Biodefense Strategy, Practice, and Science*, vol. 1, no. 2, 2003.

[4] Daniel B. Jernigam et al., "Investigation of Bioterrorism-Related Anthrax, United States, 2001: Epidemiologic Findings," *Emerging Infectious Diseases*, vol. 8, no. 10, Oct. 2002.

[5] "Parker: If You're a Terrorist and You're Happy, It Must Be March," *Salt Lake Tribune*, March 29, 2004, reprinted from the *Orlando Sentinel*.

[6] "Scores Die in Madrid Bomb Carnage," BBC News Online, March 11, 2004; http://news.bbc.co.uk/1/hi/world/europe/3500452.stm.

amounts of human resources and medical equipment to interrupt disease transmission and reduce rates of mortality through disease tracking and monitoring, verification of exposure, administration of medical countermeasures where available (for example, vaccines and preventive antibiotics), and supportive care and clinical treatment.

The case studies described herein offer a view of the challenges facing rural hospitals to meet these demands as they prepare for the threat of bioterrorism as well as non-intentional, naturally occurring epidemics of emerging contagious diseases such as severe acute respiratory syndrome (SARS). The findings are sobering and include a pervasive perception among study participants that major medical emergencies in America's rural areas and heartland would quickly overwhelm the capabilities of their small hospitals.

Many of these facilities, owing to financial restraints, are relatively old and structurally porous, incapable of containing or preventing the aerosolized spread of an infectious disease throughout the medical units and to previously non-exposed patients and health care workers. They have relatively few extras, as they are limited in medical supplies, life-sustaining equipment (such as ventilators), auxiliary power sources, and trained physicians and nurses. Communication systems across rural communities to ancillary hospital support systems (for example, police, safety and emergency medical services, and other potential sources of person-power and assistance) are unreliable and easily interrupted by terrain and weather. Most local officials acknowledge that they would be on their own for at least the first 24 to 48 hours. A catastrophic event, or an act of bioterrorism, will require that rural hospitals receive outside assistance to sustain ongoing operations, intervene in the potentially unremitting flow of medical emergencies, and contain the epidemic sequelae of a deliberately deployed pathogen. However, coordinated and reliable systems of hospital support still evade current response paradigms attributable in large part to the stovepiped streams of money and non-integrated planning efforts prevalent across the spectrum of civilian and non-civilian sectors that have identified terrorism response roles and responsibilities.

The delivery of medical care to infected populations and the containment of disease epidemics require that hospitals occupy a central role in community-based bioterrorism preparedness planning. The author provides this report to inform future initiatives to prepare America's hospitals against threats to homeland security.

Overview

The anthrax attacks of 2001 and the newly emerging global threat of severe acute respiratory syndrome (SARS) have illuminated the critical role of America's hospitals within the context of naturally occurring and deliberately disseminated microbial pathogens. In the face of increasing regulatory challenges, workforce shortages, and expanding numbers of underinsured and uninsured Americans, hospitals are expected to provide staff familiar with bioterrorist disease agents, implement protocols that prevent disease transmission to hospital personnel and patients, and participate in surveillance, reporting, and alerting strategies with other critical community responders. While these responsibilities challenge the most agile and fiscally sound of the nation's 5,000 acute-care facilities, they place a profound burden upon our roughly 2,000 rural hospitals—depending upon which definition of "rural" is applied. While rural hospitals throughout the nation have achieved various levels of preparedness, many of them remain inadequately prepared to respond to either a bioterrorist event or an outbreak of an emerging infectious disease. This lack of preparedness is a result of many factors, including limitations on general resources, inadequate resources specific to bioterrorism preparedness, and the shortage of ability and time to train hospital personnel.[1, 2, 3]

A 2003 report released by the U.S. General Accounting Office[4] on American hospitals' ability to respond to a bioterrorist attack surveyed only urban hospitals and overlooked the importance of preparedness among rural hospitals. National Rural Health Association President Wayne Myers responded, "By not taking rural hospitals and populations into consideration, the General Accounting Office is failing to acknowledge the health and safety concerns of more than 65 million Americans who call rural communities home."[5] According to the National Rural Health Association, rural areas and industries provide the majority of the nation's food and water supplies. Rural America, therefore, offers a particular vulnerability to terrorists who aim to threaten the U.S. economy. Furthermore, the majority of U.S. land bordering on Mexico and Canada supports rural communities.[6] Our porous borders, especially the 3,900-mile Canadian border, which is guarded by fewer than 400 patrol agents at a given time, present rural communities with threats of exposure to smuggled biological, chemical, radiological, and explosive weapons.[7] Rural communities may also be particularly vulnerable because of their proximity to chemical stockpiles, missile silos, and other sites that present terrorists with attractive targets.[8] Community leaders in rural areas generally acknowledge the reality of terrorist threats and trust that anticipated access to

---

[1] "What's Different About Rural Health Care?" National Rural Health Association; http://www.nrharural.org/pagefile/different.html.

[2] Thomas Rowley, "Terrorism Brings Public Health Into Focus," *Rural Health News*, winter 2002.

[3] CNN, "Small Town Fears in Face of Bioterrorism," Jan. 28, 2002; http://www.cnn.com/2002/US/01/28/counties.bioterrorism/.

[4] U.S. General Accounting Office, *Most Urban Hospitals Have Emergency Plans but Lack Certain Capacities for Bioterrorism Response*, August 2003.

[5] Rural Assistance Center, "NRHA Stresses Need for Rural Hospital Bioterrorism Preparedness," press release, Aug. 19, 2003; http://www.nrharural.org/pagefile/news/Bioterrorism.html.

[6] Thomas C. Ricketts, Karen D. Johnson Webb, and Patricia Taylor, *Definitions of Rural: A Handbook for Policy Makers and Researchers*, Federal Office of Rural Health Policy, July 1998.

[7] Bonne, Jon, "Remote Patrol: Guarding America's Back Door," MSNBC News, Sept. 30, 2003; http://www.stevequayle.com/News.alert/Canada_Mexico/020930 remote.patrol html.

[8] Associated Press, "Rural U.S. Seen a Likely Terror Target," *Billings* (MT) *Gazette*, Aug. 28, 2003.

preparedness funding would provide dual-benefit opportunities, like improvements in emergency and decontamination equipment, communications infrastructure, laboratory services, and telemedicine capabilities.[9, 10]

Perhaps one indication of the perceived threat environment is the market for terrorism insurance, which insurance companies were required to offer to all of their policyholders following the Terrorism Risk Insurance Act of 2002. Using mathematical models and information from terrorism experts, risk modelers have calculated that only 2 percent of the country's zip codes face more than 90 percent of the risk of experiencing a terrorist attack. Accordingly, the premiums for terrorism insurance in areas that these models found to be high-risk—New York City and Chicago, for example—are so high that most businesses are declining the policies. And although rural community leaders acknowledge the threat, business owners in rural areas and even smaller cities, where terrorism insurance policies are much cheaper, are not purchasing insurance. They are declining coverage because they do not perceive a risk.[11]

The potential threat of terrorist attacks in rural American communities stems from the attractive targets presented by those components of our critical infrastructure that are most concentrated in rural areas. Particularly vulnerable to biosecurity threats are the agriculture and food production industries, which contribute $1.24 trillion to the U.S. economy annually and account for one in eight American jobs.[12] In 2002, Secretary of Agriculture Ann Veneman testified before the U.S. Senate Committee on Agriculture, Nutrition and Forestry regarding the her department's vital role in homeland security, with responsibility "to better protect agriculture, our food supply and consumers from potential terrorist threats."[13] Reacting to the urgency of the post-9/11 threat environment, the Department of Agriculture initiated a series of exercises in late 2002 to illustrate barriers to biosecurity preparedness for agricultural terrorism, or agroterrorism. The first simulation, "Crimson Sky," demonstrated that a deliberately deployed outbreak of foot-and-mouth disease, which is caused by a highly contagious virus that infects all cloven-hoofed animals, presents a grave threat to the security and economic stability of the United States. The second simulation, "Crimson Guard," examined the operational issues revealed in Crimson Sky, involving federal and state animal health and emergency response officials. The third, "Crimson Winter," was designed to examine issues specifically related to the Food Safety and Inspection Service.[14]

"Today's world poses unprecedented new threats to U.S. agriculture," states a February 2004 press release from the U.S. Department of Homeland Security. "While inspections have traditionally focused on

---

[9] Connie Jo Discoe, "Heineman: Other States Envy Nebraska's Efforts on Homeland Security," *McCook Daily Gazette,* Jan. 13, 2004.

[10] Oklahoma State University Center for Health Sciences, "OSU Grant Boosts Rural Health Care Response to Bioterrorism Threats," *Communications: News and Events*, Oct. 27, 2003; http://www healthsciences.okstate.edu/center/support/communi/press_release/2003.10.27_ruralhealthgrant html.

[11] Diane Brady, "Commentary: Terrorism: Put the Money Where the Danger Is," *Business Week Online*, April 14, 2003; http://www.businessweek.com/magazine/content/03_15/b3828618.htm.

[12] Peter Chalk, "Hitting America's Soft Underbelly: The Potential Threat of Deliberate Biological Attacks Against the U.S. Agricultural and Food Industry," RAND Corporation, 2004.

[13] Testimony of Ann M. Veneman, Secretary of Agriculture, before the U.S. Senate Committee on Agriculture, Nutrition and Forestry, July 17, 2002; http://www.usda.gov/news/special/ctc31 htm.

[14] The Department of Agriculture commissioned ANSER to conduct these exercises (Food Safety and Inspection Service, U.S. Department of Agriculture, "Perspectives on Food Security." See also remarks prepared for delivery by Dr. Elsa Murano, Under Secretary for Food Safety, before the Association of Contingency Planners forum, titled "Best Practices in Business Continuity: A Global Perspective from the Nation's Capital," co-sponsored by the U.S. Department of Agriculture Grad School, Oct. 29, 2003, Washington, DC.

accidental introduction of harmful pests and diseases, a post–September 11 world demands that we also focus on the deliberate introduction of these threats."[15] This press release followed on the heels of President Bush's announcement of Homeland Security Presidential Directive 9, which acknowledges that the nation's "agriculture and food system is an extensive, open, interconnected, diverse, and complex structure providing potential targets for terrorist attacks" and calls for the establishment of "a national policy to defend the agriculture and food system against terrorist attacks, major disasters, and other emergencies." Clearly, acts of agroterrorism using non-zoonotic agents such as foot-and-mouth disease pose little if any threat to human health and would require a veterinary, not necessarily medical, response. However, threats to such a key component of our critical infrastructure in turn compromise civil order and the safety of citizens in rural communities, justifying efforts to strengthen medical response capabilities in those communities. Non-zoonotic infectious diseases and other concerns not specific to biosecurity, such as nuclear facilities, chemical plants, and military installations, pose direct threats to human health and therefore support cogent arguments for the need to improve rural hospital preparedness capabilities.

---

[15] U.S. Department of Homeland Security press release, "Protecting Against Agricultural Terrorism," Feb. 2, 2004; http://www.dhs.gov/dhspublic/display?content=3117.

Background

As rural hospitals acknowledge their vulnerabilities and prepare for the threats of bioterrorism and emerging microbial diseases, the relationships among rural communities, their health care providers, and policy makers augur a climate of deliberation, altered business practices, and changed fiscal demands. Rural communities have unique vulnerabilities and population and infrastructure characteristics, which pose unprecedented challenges to rural hospitals as the demands of bioterrorism preparedness and response are considered and addressed. Some of the greatest concerns include alerting remote and dispersed populations to threats and augmenting limited hospital facilities and human resources to meet the demands of an epidemic or a mass-casualty medical emergency magnified by limited transportation and communications infrastructures. In this context, policy changes and funding deliberations must occur to shape the preparedness efforts of rural communities and their hospitals.

Defining the "Rural" Community Poses Policy and Funding Challenges

In preparing to alert populations to a threat and intervene during a health emergency, such as an event of bioterrorism, it is important to understand the demographic distinctions among populations that may signal unique preparedness needs. For example, the definitions that designate communities as "rural" are inconsistent.

The impediments that geographical isolation places on patient transport and emergency response are exacerbated by severe weather for long periods in many parts of the country. In some of these areas, the mountainous terrain disrupts communications as well.

One of the key findings of a July 2002 Department of Health and Human Services Rural Task Force report, *One Department Serving Rural America,* was that the absence of a common, interagency-wide definition of "rural," as well as the lack of a more precise gradient between "rural" and "urban," makes it difficult for governments to target grants, evaluate services, and develop policies to benefit the broad spectrum of rural communities. In general, the U.S. Census Bureau uses the term "rural" to classify regions containing populations of 2,500 people or fewer, or unincorporated areas with population densities below 1,000 people per square mile. The census classifies all that is not "urban" as rural. Consequently, areas that are designated "rural" can vary widely from areas with one or two persons per square mile to areas with 999 persons per square mile. The U.S. Office of Management and Budget uses the term "non-metropolitan" to indicate rural areas and populations. "Non-metropolitan" refers to counties that do not meet minimum population requirements, do not contain a central metropolitan area, or are otherwise not associated closely with urban areas. The Office of Management and Budget makes these designations on the county level because, historically, population data are reported at the county level.[1] Approximately 72 percent of the 3,140 U.S. counties are grouped into the non-metropolitan category.[2] Although there is considerable overlap between the Census Bureau and the Office of Management and Budget classification systems, they do not completely coincide.

In addition to definitional distinctions, rural populations can be characterized by their racial delineations. The racial composition of rural populations tends to be more homogenous than in urban populations, but demographics vary greatly among sub-regions of the nation. For example, rural African Americans are most concentrated in the Southern and Southeast Atlantic States, Native Americans are most concentrated in the Four Corners region, the Northern Great Plains, and Oklahoma, and Hispanics are most concentrated in the Southwest states.[3] Such disparities may require variations in health services from region to region based on ethnic, linguistic, or cultural differences that are not taken into account by current policy strategies targeting rural populations.

America's largely rural food and agriculture industry, which contributes $1.24 trillion to the U.S. economy annually and accounts for one in eight American jobs, is particularly vulnerable to terrorist attack.[4]

---

[1] A metropolitan area as defined by the Office of Management and Budget consists of a densely populated core area and adjacent counties that are economically and socially integrated with the core area; it must include at least one city with 50,000 or more inhabitants or a Census Bureau–defined urbanized area (with a population of at least 50,000) and a total metropolitan population of at least 100,000 (Ricketts et. al, *Definitions of Rural: A Handbook for Policy Makers and Researchers*, Federal Office of Rural Health Policy, July 1998).

[2] National Advisory Committee on Rural Health, *A Targeted Look at the Rural Healthcare Safety Net*, 2002.

[3] Rural Policy Research Institute, *Rural by the Numbers: Information about Rural America*, data from 1990; http://www.rupri.org/resources/rnumbers/demopop/demo.html#Map percent205.

[4] "Hitting America's Soft Underbelly: The Potential Threat of Deliberate Biological Attacks Against the U.S. Agricultural and Food Industry," RAND Corporation, 2004.

According to the National Rural Health Association, the residents of rural areas, who make up 20 percent of the U.S. population, are far more likely than urban residents to die if they experience motor vehicle accidents, unintentional injuries, or gunshot wounds. Elderly individuals and obese individuals make up a greater proportion of the rural population than the urban population. Rates of alcohol and tobacco use are higher in rural counties. Chronic illnesses and suicides are more prevalent in rural areas, and it is more common for rural adults to describe their health status as fair or poor. Both male and female death rates are considerably higher in rural areas than in urban areas.[5] In recent years, rural communities throughout the country have suffered from epidemic rates of methamphetamine use and related health problems, including exposure to the toxic chemicals involved in methamphetamine production.[6]

Limited surge capacity is one of the most pressing issues in preparing rural hospitals for mass-casualty events. Hospitals in rural areas tend to be small and resource-strapped, and thus are likely to find it difficult to address large-scale health emergencies.[7]

---

[5] "What's Different About Rural Health Care?" National Rural Health Association; http://www.nrharural.org/pagefile/different.html.

[6] Fox Butterfield, "Across Rural Midwest, Drug Casts a Grim Shadow," *New York Times*, Jan. 4, 2004.

[7] "Optimizing Surge Capacity: Regional Efforts in Bioterrorism Readiness," Agency for Healthcare Research and Quality, January 2004.

Existing Workforce Shortages and Barriers to Health Care Access May Impact Rural Hospital Preparedness and Response Efforts

Rural hospitals have filled an important niche in providing primary care and community health services, but they must rely on a "stabilize and transport" model if patients require complex tertiary care.

Workforce and health service capacities have been identified as major issues in hospital preparedness efforts in both urban and rural settings. Although rural communities have an obvious need for a full spectrum of health services commensurate with those offered to urban communities, current reports indicate that these areas remain relatively underserved by the medical community. Because rural areas tend to have about half as many physicians per capita as urban areas, nearly 75 percent of rural counties have regions that are designated as medically underserved areas,[8] and rural areas are nearly four times more likely to be designated Health Professional Shortage Areas (one primary care physician per at least 3,500 residents) than are metropolitan areas.[9] Rural populations tend to suffer from a significant shortage of medical specialists as well: nearly 90 percent of all specialists practice in urban areas. Rural Americans are also less likely to receive routine dental care as well. Rising malpractice insurance premiums, particularly in high-risk specialties like obstetrics, are exacerbating the shortage of medical specialists in rural areas.[10] There are fewer mental health professionals per capita practicing in rural areas, and rural hospitals are far less likely than urban hospitals to provide emergency mental health care.[11] The provision of emergency medical services in rural communities is relatively limited.[12]

---

[8] Kaiser Commission on Medicaid and the Uninsured, "The Uninsured in Rural America," 2003.

[9] Federal Office of Rural Health Policy, "Facts about Rural Physicians," Sept. 1997; http://www.shepscenter.unc.edu/research_programs/rural_program/phy html

[10] Thomas D. Rowley, "High Insurance Premiums Jeopardize Rural OBs," *Rural Health News*, vol. 9, no. 1, spring-summer 2002.

[11] "What's Different About Rural Health Care?" National Rural Health Association; http://www.nrharural.org/pagefile/different html

[12] National Rural Health Association, "Rural and Frontier Emergency Medical Services Toward the Year 2000," 1997.

The high rates of poverty found in rural communities contribute to a variety of health problems and diminished access to quality health care and health insurance.

Rural residents are not only relatively more underserved by the medical community than their metropolitan counterparts, they also have greater difficulties accessing health care providers. For example, the frequently limited or absent public transportation infrastructure in rural communities impedes general population mobility as well as travel to reach a hospital or a physician for routine or urgent care.[13, 14] Presenting a greater barrier to health care access and preparedness in rural communities is the limited versatility of rural hospitals in providing care and expanded services as compared to their urban counterparts. Geographic isolation, limited specialized medical services, and a generally constrained budget often render rural hospitals unable to provide care in the just-in-time manner of urban hospitals and emergency facilities. For a number of reasons, rural hospitals tend to be more poorly equipped and less versatile in treating patients than urban and suburban hospitals. Rural hospitals also have lower profit margins, which limits their abilities to attract investors, make improvements, and maintain stocks of supplies. A study conducted at the University of Minnesota Rural Health Research Center found that capital investment in rural hospitals failed to prove profitable for investors, and therefore most investments are made in the form of charity.[15] These charitable investments are not sustainable solutions, however, and are rarely sufficient for significantly improving medical services and maintaining supply reserves. Although an increasing number of urban residents have opted to move out of metropolitan areas to rural communities, the rural health care system has not seen the financial and strategic investments necessary to sustain its viability. Urban sprawl has thus placed greater burdens on the rural health care infrastructure.[16]

---

[13] "What's Different About Rural Health Care?"

[14] Department of Health and Human Services Rural Task Force, report to the Secretary: *One Department Serving Rural America*, 2002.

[15] Jeffrey Stensland et al., "Rate of Return on Capital Investments at Small Rural Hospitals, "University of Minnesota Rural Health Research Center Working Paper #45, Jan. 2003.

[16] Laurent Belsie, "Rural America's New Problem: Handling Sprawl," *Christian Science Monitor*, Dec. 10, 2002; http://www.csmonitor.com/2002/1210/p03s01-ussc.html

Widespread poverty and a limited availability of health insurance also continue to impede access to health care in rural areas and strain relations between communities and health care providers. On the average, per capita income in rural America is $7,417 lower than in urban areas. Rural workers are twice as likely to earn minimum wage, and they are less likely to advance in employment status over time.[17] Rural individuals are more likely to live below the poverty line; 14 percent of rural Americans, and nearly 24 percent of rural children, live in poverty. These factors place rural residents at a great disadvantage in affording personal health insurance for themselves and their families. Unfortunately, rural areas have fewer large employers who are willing and able to absorb some of the cost of health insurance for their employees. Rural workers are more likely to work for small businesses and are less likely to be offered health benefits from employers.[18] In 1999, up to seven percent of rural counties had no access to coverage by any health maintenance organization.[19] In these counties, even employers wishing to offer health insurance to employees would not be able to do so. It is common throughout the health care industry, in both rural and urban settings, for insurance plans to deny coverage for mental health care.[20] The difficulty in affording and obtaining private insurance can be seen in the data showing that only 60 percent of rural non-elderly residents have private insurance, while 72 percent of the non-elderly population in urban communities is privately insured.[21]

Rural Hospitals Face Daunting Fiscal Restraints in a New Climate of Threats

Before the 20th century, only a limited number of hospitals existed in the United States. Those who could not receive adequate home care, including urban workers displaced from family, immigrants, dependants, and the indigent and poor, sought medical attention at almshouses, which had become municipal hospitals in function, if not in name, but which offered few services and procedures. With the growth of scientific knowledge, technology, and medical expertise toward the early 1900s, however, hospitals became focal points of the emerging medical enterprise. By 1909, there were 4,359 hospitals in the United States, both public and private,[22] containing 421,065 beds. All sectors of American society sought treatment in hospitals when necessary. With increasing dependence on technology and the growing competence of medical capabilities in treating illness, American hospitals required paying patients to provide a more robust financial base. Paying patients had previously played a minor role amid minimal state and municipal funds, small endowments, and community fundraising activities in financing early hospitals. Private hospitals took on the role of competing for paying customers by offering hospitality, private

---

[17] Brad Gibbens, "Rural Hospital Flexibility Program: Moving Forward," presented to the 2003 July Trustee Conference, Leadership and Accountability in Health Care, Minnesota Hospital Association, July 12, 2003.

[18] Kaiser Commission on Medicaid and the Uninsured, "The Uninsured in Rural America," 2003.

[19] Timothy McBride, Courtney Andrews, Keith Miller, and Michael Shambaugh-Miller, "An Analysis of Availability of Medicare + Choice, Commercial HMO, and FEHBP Plans in Rural Areas: Implications for Medicare Reform," Rural Policy Research Institute, *Rural Policy Brief*, vol. 8, no. 5, March 2003.

[20] *Rural Communities and Emergency Preparedness*, Office of Rural Health Policy, Health Resources and Services Administration, and the U.S. Department of Health and Human Services, April 2002.

[21] Kaiser Commission on Medicaid and the Uninsured, "The Uninsured in Rural America."

[22] Public hospitals are operated and supported by elected governing bodies while private hospitals are owned and managed by a legal entity other than a government agency. With respect to management and ownership, private hospitals fall into two general categories: for-profit or not-for profit. For-profit hospitals are owned by investors, to whom profits are returned; not-for profit hospitals are owned by non-public corporations and are typically run by a boards of trustees. Not-for-profit hospitals are also exempt from federal tax requirements and use their profits to cover capital expenses and future operating costs (Alabama Hospital Association, Hospital Terminology; http://www.alaha.org/terms.pdf).

rooms for patients, and the latest treatment and diagnostic procedures, while public hospitals, for the most part, continued to provide medical care for the poor.[23] Hospitals had become the most economically feasible way to provide health care to communities, but by the 1930s, the cost of hospital care had risen so high that it became unattainable to the middle class—it seemed that only the wealth of the rich or the dignity of the poor could elicit hospital care.[24] Private insurance emerged as way for the middle class to access hospital care, which was now the dominant venue for health care in general.[25] When healthcare costs became even higher, federal assistance programs emerged, including Medicaid and Medicare in the 1960s, to cover patients previously covered by charity.

As traditional providers for the poor, America's network of large urban municipal hospitals has become a major component of our health care safety net, which acts as the default health care provider for the nation's nearly 44 million uninsured individuals.[26] The health care safety net includes not only the large urban municipal institutions commonly associated with public health care, but also the network of smaller public and not-for-profit hospitals built under the Hill-Burton Act of 1946 in rural communities, where 20 percent of uninsured Americans live today.[27] As components of this safety net, all of these hospitals rely on payments from the Medicaid and Medicare programs for revenue. Unfortunately, because of the ways in which costs are reported to federal programs, rates of Medicaid and Medicare reimbursement to rural hospitals and physicians are often dramatically lower than those to their urban counterparts for equivalent services.[28, 29, 30] Note that the Medicare Prescription Drug, Improvement and Modernization Act of 2003, Title IV, "Rural Provisions," aims to stabilize the financial environment of the rural heath care system by increasing Medicare reimbursements to rural health care workers and hospitals. The bill stipulates that hospital payment rates from Medicare will increase each year over the next four years and aims to equalize payment rates between rural and urban hospitals.[31]

Several attempts have been made to improve the financial conditions in which rural hospitals operate. The Balanced Budget Act of 1997, for example, created the federally assisted Medicare Rural Hospital Flexibility Program. This program set up efficient rural health care networks consisting of at least one

---

[23] Charles E. Rosenberg, *The Care of Strangers: The Rise of America's Hospital System* (New York: Basic Books, 1987).

[24] Rosenberg, 1987.

[25] J. Rogers and Ellen Jane Hollingsworth, *Controversy About American Hospitals* (Washington, DC: American Enterprise Institute for Public Policy Research, 1987).

[26] Institute of Medicine, *America's Health Care Safety Net*, 2000.

[27] Kaiser Commission on Medicaid and the Uninsured. "The Uninsured in Rural America."

[28] "What's Different About Rural Health Care?" National Rural Health Association; http://www.nrharural.org/pagefile/different.html.

[29] Rural Health Advisory Committee, Minnesota Department of Health, "Rural and Urban Reimbursement: Hospitals, Nursing Homes, and the Minnesota Advantage Health Plan," Jan. 22, 2002; http://www.health.state.mn.us/divs/chs/rhac/reimbmulder.htm.

[30] Note that the Medicare Prescription Drug, Improvement and Modernization Act of 2003, Title IV, "Rural Provisions," aims to stabilize the financial environment of the rural heath care system by increasing Medicare reimbursements to rural health care workers and hospitals. The bill stipulated that hospital payment rates from Medicare would increase each year over the next four years and aimed to equalize payment rates between rural and urban hospitals (James Ahrens, "Guest Opinion: Medicare Bill Helps Rural Hospitals," *Billings* [MT] *Gazette*, Nov. 21, 2003).

[31] Penny E. Mohr et al., "The Financial Dependence of Rural Hospitals on Outpatient Revenue," Project Hope Walsh Center for Rural Health Analysis, 1998.

critical access hospital and one full-service hospital under certain agreements regarding patient referral and transfer, communications, and patient transportation.[32] A critical access hospital is an acute care facility that is downsized by reducing services to minimize the per-patient operational costs of the hospital, and the rural networks are designed to reduce transport costs, which add considerably to operational costs.[33, 34] However, by implementing a prospective payment system for outpatient services in hospitals, the act greatly constrained the ability of rural hospitals to generate revenue from outpatient services and, therefore, negatively impacted the hospitals' ability to financially support other services, including inpatient care.

As part of its initiative to revitalize and resource the strained rural health care system, the Department of Health and Human Services allocated $46 million in federal grants for the funding of rural and frontier hospitals across the country for 2003. These grants came in the form of $23 million through the Medicare Rural Hospital Flexibility program, which is designed to directly augment the reimbursements for rural health services, and $8 million in grants directly payable to state governments to further improve the rural health care system through technical support and workforce recruitment, among other things.[35] Another $15 million is allocated to hospitals with fewer than 50 beds through the Small Hospital Improvement Program to help pay for costs related to prospective payment system implementation and improve their service standards.[36]

Rural Hospital Preparedness for Bioterrorism

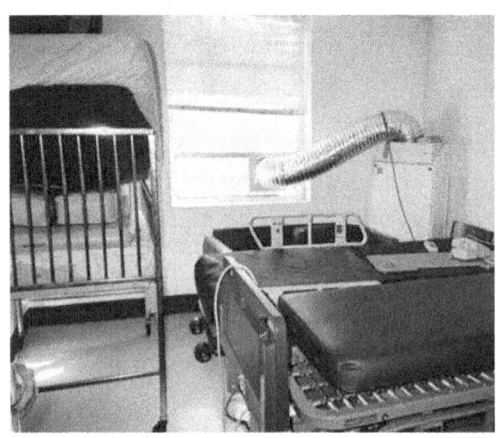

Makeshift isolation facilities, like this one found at one of this study's participating hospitals, will offer little protection to the hospital's workforce and patients in the event of bioterrorism or an infectious disease outbreak.

In response to the terrorist attacks that occurred in the fall of 2001, the Health Resources and Services Administration distributed $125 million in federal funds during 2002 to prepare hospitals for mass-casualty events, particularly bioterrorism. In 2003, the level of funding increased to $498 million, and $515 million has been allocated to the program for 2004. The President's Budget request for 2005 is $476 million, which reflects an 8 percent reduction from the funding allocated in 2004. The funds from

[32] U.S. Department of Health and Human Services. "Rural Hospitals, Health Care Systems Strengthened by $13 Million in Grant Awards," press release, Sept. 10, 1999; http://www.hhs.gov/news/press/1999pres/990910.html

[33] Robert Berenson, testimony on the Balanced budget act and rural hospitals before the Senate Appropriations Subcommittee on Agriculture, Rural Development, and Related Agencies, July 11, 2000.

[34] Health and Human Services Rural Task Force, report to the Secretary: *One Department Serving Rural America.* 2002.

[35] Department of Health and Human Services, "HHS Takes New Steps to Promote Quality Health Care and Social Services in Rural America," press release, July 26, 2002.

[36] Premier, Inc., "HHS Announces Availability of $15 Million in Grant Funding for Rural Hospitals; Application Deadline Is June 21," *Advocacy News,* June 5, 2002; http://www.premierinc.com/frames/index.jsp?pagelocation=/all/advocacy/issues/107th/2002/other/rural-grant-funding-0602 htm.

the Health Resources and Services Administration are accompanied by federal guidance that highlights priority areas for improvement, which include surge capacity, emergency medical services, linkages to public health departments, education and preparedness training, and terrorism preparedness exercises.[37, 38, 39]

The Joint Commission on Accreditation of Healthcare Organizations (JCAHO), a national accrediting body that has accredited 4,644 hospitals as of 2002,[40] has echoed these preparedness priorities. According to the JCAHO Emergency Management Standards, each accredited healthcare organization is required to have an emergency management plan and must conduct drills regularly, at least twice per year, to test the plan. The JCAHO standards outline the required components of an emergency management plan that addresses mitigation, preparedness, response, and recovery. The standards require organizations to define their vulnerabilities, coordinate with other community responders, and define roles for individuals and the organization as a whole.[41] Updated in 2001, JCAHO's Emergency Management Standards now reflect expanded expectations to prepare entire communities for disaster response rather than focusing only on preparing healthcare organizations. According to a 2003 report by JCAHO, however, community-wide preparedness plans are very rare, and almost all exist in large metropolitan areas.[42]

The Secretary of Health and Human Services has included the state offices of rural health, which act as advocates for state rural health concerns, in guiding and advising the Department of Health and Human Services Bioterrorism Preparedness Program. This program directs federal funding at improving the capacity of hospitals to respond to bioterrorist attacks and other disease outbreaks or mass-casualty events. An April 2002 study titled *Rural Communities and Emergency Preparedness* by the Office of Rural Health Policy within the Health Resources and Services Administration reported questionnaire results from 32 state offices of rural health regarding rural emergency preparedness among the states. All responding states were developing or revising terrorism response plans. Several of the state offices of rural health noted that their states faced difficulties in coordinating plans between the state government and tribal nations and that the statewide plans failed to target the specific needs and vulnerabilities of rural healthcare providers. These difficulties were unique to preparing rural communities and healthcare infrastructures for response to terrorism. Only five of the responding state offices indicated that their states had adequate epidemiologic surveillance capacity. Most of the other state offices responded that their health systems would require more robust funding, increased workforce, and other resources in order to achieve and maintain adequate surveillance and response capabilities. State offices responded

---

[37] Health Resources and Services Administration annual report for fiscal year 2002; http://www.hrsa.gov/annualreport/part5 htm.

[38] Department of Health and Human Services, "Guidelines for Bioterrorism Funding Announced," press release, May 9, 2003.

[39] Department of Health and Human Services: Budget in Brief, FY 2005; http://www.hhs.gov/budget/05budget/fy2005bibfinal.pdf.

[40] Established as an independent, not-for-profit organization in 1951, JCAHO is the nation's predominant standards-setting and accrediting body in U.S. health care. JCAHO's standards address an organization's level of performance in key functional areas, such as patient rights, patient treatment, and infection control. A competitive edge in the health care market, accreditation is earned and maintained by meeting standards in many areas and paying for onsite surveys by JCAHO survey teams every three years; http://www.jcaho.org/about+us/index.htm.

[41] JCAHO, Emergency Management Standards—EC.1.4 and EC.2.9.1; http://www.jcrinc.com/subscribers/perspectives.asp?durki=2914&site=10&return=2897.

[42] *Health Care at the Crossroads: Strategies for Creating and Sustaining Community-Wide Emergency Preparedness Systems*, JCAHO, 2003; http://www.jcaho.org/news+room/press+kits/emergency+prep htm.

overwhelmingly that the current response infrastructure for a terrorist or bioterrorist attack was either very limited or nonexistent in the rural areas of their states. Some respondents expressed concerns that a significant barrier to preparedness is complacency and the belief that rural communities are not at risk.[43]

Rural American communities are far from isolated. Of the 3-million-mile network of arterial, collector, and local roads in the United States, which links rural and urban areas and carries freight, food, health-care and other goods and services, 78 percent is in rural areas. Additionally, tourism and recreation industries such as skiing have now become prime economic drivers in rural communities previously dependent on timber, mining, and agriculture.[44]

---

[43] *Rural Communities and Emergency Preparedness*, Office of Rural Health Policy, Health Resources and Services Administration, and the U.S. Department of Health and Human Services, April 2002.

[44] "Transportation—Invest in America: Local Roads and Bridges"; http://www.transportation.org/bottomline/highways05 html.

Study Methodology

This study was conducted to investigate hospital preparedness for mass-casualty—specifically biological—emergencies in America's rural communities. "Rural" counties are defined to be "non-metropolitan" counties, as determined by the Office of Management and Budget. Non-metropolitan counties have no urban centers and are not economically dependent upon adjacent or nearby urban centers. Dependence is said to be established when 25 percent of the employed population of a county commutes to an urban center or when 25 percent of a county's working population comprises residents of an urban center. To be classified as an urban area upon which another county can be characterized as dependent, the U.S. Census Bureau requires a population density of 1,000 persons per square mile.[1]

Within rural communities, and for the purpose of this study, potential hospitals were selected for participation if they met the criteria of having one or more vulnerability factors that may augment a community's value as a strategic terrorist target. Vulnerability factors included proximity to military installations, nuclear or chemical plants, large-scale agricultural production, an international border, or major waterways. Additionally, hospitals were selected to represent five geographic regions of the country: the Northwest, Southwest, Northeast, Southeast, and Midwest.

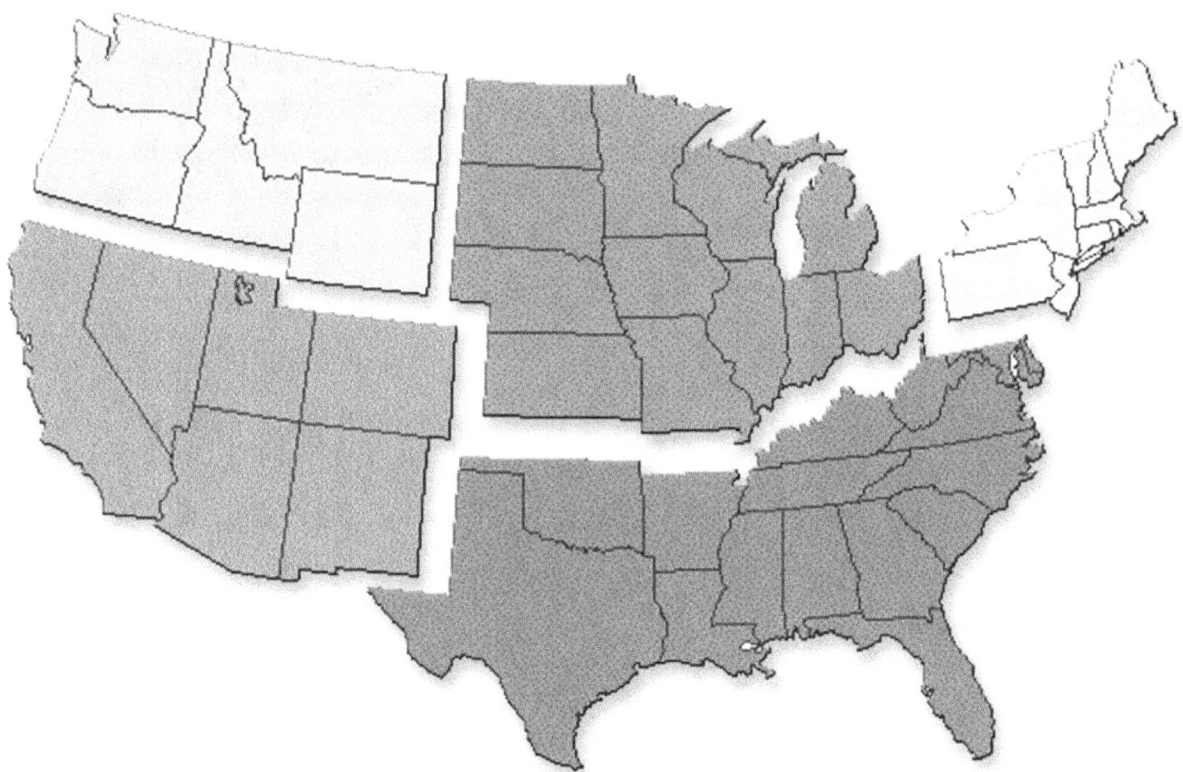

To ensure diversity and national representation among participating organizations, this study enrolled rural hospitals from each of the five major regions of the United States.

The intent of this study was to visit and gather data from five hospitals, one in each of those geographic regions. An initial pool of 11 hospitals was selected, and each hospital was mailed a letter of introduction explaining the study. After subsequent phone calls assessing levels of interest among the hospitals, five were selected for participation. For security reasons, all participating hospitals were promised that they would not be identified by name or location in any final or summary reports and that any specific comments made by any participants during the meetings would not be attributed in a way that would identify the contributor. All site visits and meetings were conducted during December 2003.

Two-day site visits at each hospital involved meetings with "decision-making personnel," including chief executive officers, chief operating officers, chief medical officers and facility directors; "department personnel," such as trauma coordinators and emergency department medical and nursing directors; elected officials; and representatives from the traditional responder community including firefighters, police officers, and emergency medical technicians (EMTs). These meetings were supplemented with a tour of the hospital facility, intended to clarify information discussed in the interviews.

The interview instrument was consistently employed for all five onsite visits. It was tested and refined prior to use. The interview was designed to consist of only open-ended discussion questions. Follow-up questions that were aimed at elucidating specifics of the bioterrorism preparedness plans were posed by the principal investigator as needed through the course of the conversation. Specific probative questions were noted in typed transcripts of the interviews. Each hospital CEO was given the opportunity to review for accuracy and approve the written hospital profile.

Hospitals were given an honorarium for their role in coordinating meetings with hospital and non-hospital participants and to cover the costs of refreshments supplied during the meetings.

---

[1] Economic Research Service, USDA. "Measuring Rurality: What Is Rural?"; http://www.ers.usda.gov/briefing/rurality/WhatisRural/.

Findings

Hospital One Profile

Hospital One is a 40-year-old facility, operated and supported by the county government, that eliminated half its beds two years ago to achieve designation as a critical access hospital. The hospital provides medical care to a catchment population of approximately 10,000 persons, of which 97 percent are native English speakers. Forty percent of the population is over age 65. The mean annual household income is $33,000.

Agriculture is the dominant industry in the community served by Hospital One, which is located within a nexus of roadways supporting heavy transcontinental trucking. Over the past several years there has been a subtle influx of foreign (predominantly Asian) ownership and labor into the local agricultural industry, which houses a portion of the nation's meatpacking industry and produces soybeans, corn, cattle, pigs, and poultry. Hospital One is also proximate to a nuclear power plant. Nuclear facility representatives engage in required annual drills[1] with the hospital but acknowledged that they have become interested in developing better communication and relationships with the hospital since the events of 9/11. The nuclear facility has received $10 million to upgrade security measures, including communications and employee background checks. As area residents and birthright farmers, many of the nuclear facility workers—as well as the emergency responders who participated in the study discussions—noted that they are equally concerned about the threat of agroterrorism. As one participant noted, "If they can fly planes into buildings they can come into a feed lot and contaminate the feed." Aware of the agriculture industry's severe vulnerability to outbreaks of infectious animal disease, another emergency responder noted, "Contaminate one [grain] elevator and you will contaminate all cattle."

A report analyzing the relationship between the health of the county's citizens and the health of the county's economy helped support passage of a hospital bond in 2001, resulting in a 10-bed renovation that included a new rehabilitation facility, remodeled operating room, emergency room, and outpatient facilities, and a new business office. Twenty-one visiting medical specialists support a variety of outpatient clinical services. The hospital employs 16 full-time registered nurses and four licensed practical nurses. They have a 24-hour emergency department supported by an ambulance service and capabilities of transporting patients by helicopter. Hospital One has a single-bed isolation room equipped with negative-pressure airflow capacity. However, hospital administrators cannot validate how the isolation room's negative-airflow capacity has been tested and are not sure the nurses know how to operate the facility.

---

[1] Following the accident at Three Mile Island in 1979, the Nuclear Regulatory Commission reexamined the role of emergency planning for protection of the public in the vicinity of nuclear power plants. The commission issued regulations requiring that before a plant could be licensed to operate, the commission must have "reasonable assurance that adequate protective measures can and will be taken in the event of a radiological emergency." The regulations require that comprehensive emergency plans be prepared and periodically exercised to assure that actions can and will be taken to notify and protect citizens in the vicinity of a nuclear facility. Typically the emergency preparedness plan for a nuclear power plant includes an area within about a 10-mile radius around the plant. The facility's emergency response plan must be discussed and agreed upon by the organization operating the power plant, by local and county emergency response officials, and by state emergency management officials; http://www.nrc.gov.

Administrators and staff have considered many critical preparedness questions ("How would we protect the hospital's resources in the event of a surge in demand? Under what circumstances can the hospital lock its doors? Where would additional trained resources come from? How would we resupply blood and critical medical equipment?"), but potential solutions have not been resolved. Pediatric training and equipment are limited, and personnel have very little experience in the large-scale triage and tagging procedures necessary during a mass-casualty event. In the event of bioterrorism, there is an expectation among law enforcement and safety personnel that the sheriff would institute a "code red" and instruct emergency medical services to suit up. A flattened decision-making paradigm has been instituted so that individuals on duty during weekends and evenings can act expeditiously during a serious or potentially contagious situation. A large influx of patients presenting with complex medical conditions would quickly overwhelm hospital capacities and capabilities.

Terrorism and infectious diseases have been objects of great concern among hospital staff members over the past three years. The hospital administrator suspects that these and other concerns have not gone unnoticed by the insurance industry, reporting "extreme increases" in the cost of property coverage exceeding 15 percent per year. The nursing staff notes greater sensitivity to unusual events, stating that they now contact the police far more readily if they perceive anything to be out of the ordinary. As time has passed since the 2001 anthrax attacks, the hospital has considered the threat of bioterrorism less of a "front burner" issue, replaced by the more recent concerns of SARS, West Nile virus, and influenza. (Hospital staff members recall a time when all hospital beds were filled to capacity during a large flu outbreak.)

Hospital One belongs to a statewide consortium of 30 hospitals, most of which are rural and lack JCAHO accreditation. The consortium has initiated writing multi-hospital agreements for assistance in the event of an emergency. An appraisal of this assistance strategy, along with many other lessons learned, was made after Hospital One participated in a small tabletop exercise with several nearby hospitals. For example, in discussing the generalizability of her skills during an emergency if deployed to assist another hospital, one nurse noted, "We don't know Pyxis[2] at our hospital and we do our meds differently."

Hospital One has actively sought to determine how to augment its limited personnel capacity in the event of a large-scale emergency. Currently, maintenance workers function as security guards when needed, although they have had no security training. There has been some work with ministerial personnel to supplement mental health services in the event of a crisis. The hospital has agreements with nursing homes to provide additional surge capacity, but these scenarios have not been practiced. There is agreement that resources are inadequate to independently distribute supplies from the Strategic National Stockpile.[3] In the event of an emergency, the hospital would have limited support from volunteers who are described as being "the same twenty or thirty people who already wear multiple hats."

---

[2] Pyxis Medstation is one of the automated medication-dispensing system that entered hospitals during the 1980s to reduce rates of medication error, increase workforce efficiency, and improve patient safety, pharmacy inventory, and billing processes. It resembles an automatic teller machine, but it dispenses medications on the nursing unit after a physician electronically enters orders into the system. Each nurse with access to the system requires a unique code (*Making Health Care Safer: A Critical Analysis of Patient Safety Practices*, Evidence Report/Technology Assessment: Number 43, Agency for Healthcare Research and Quality Publication No. 01-E058, July 2001; http://www.ahrq.gov/clinic/ptsafety).

[3] In 1999, the Department of Health and Human Services designed and established the National Pharmaceutical Stockpile to provide a rapid (within 12 hours of the federal decision to deploy) resupply of large quantities of essential medical materiel to states and communities in the event of an emergency. Following the Homeland

One participant noted that not all consortium hospitals have been equally convinced of the climate of threats and vulnerabilities. This participant acted accordingly and described the following scenario: "The rail line went through the town [of one dubious hospital administrator] so I got the list of what has been transported on the Union Pacific over the past three months. His eyes opened real wide and he got interested in preparedness real quick."

It was suggested that both limited resources and the camaraderie inherent in a small rural hospital negate the use of relatively basic infection control practices. For example, surgical masks are not routinely worn when a patient with an upper respiratory infection presents in the emergency department. "We know the patients who come in," noted one nurse. "They're our family and friends. They get offended if we put [exam] gloves on."

Training tops the list of needs expressed by the majority of participants. One participant noted, "There is a dire need for [both] good training and consistent retraining to maintain skills." Staff indicated that they need training in bioagents, detection and increased awareness, and incident command. They note the requirement for numerous exercises to test roles and "give the staff the tools to do their job." Releasing staff from work responsibilities to acquire training—should it become available—is a significant obstacle.

Communications—systems and equipment—was another requirement reiterated by the meeting participants over the two-day site visit. Public health funding has supported the installation of fax and Internet equipment within every hospital in the state. This equipment is monitored by a hospital nurse at all times. The staff indicated that the most critical communications necessities included equipment that is both reliable and interoperable across sectors and radio capability to communicate with local, state, and federal agencies. "Lots of parts of the state still have dial-up modems," one participant noted.

Hospital Two Profile

Hospital Two serves a catchment population of which 70 percent does not use English as its primary language. Forty percent of the population is over age 65. The hospital provides care to both the indigenous population as well as many undocumented persons in need of health services. Ties between the hospital and the community are strong. Almost everyone who works at the hospital has a family member who is also employed there, fostering a strong sense of loyalty.

A 93-bed hospital in which 76 are staffed, the facility has had four major renovations since it was built in 1959. The most recent renovation in 2002 upgraded the emergency and radiology departments, the pharmacy, the lobby and administrative offices, and the outpatient clinics. The hospital is seeking capitalization to expand its facility to meet a growing demand for service delivery, to upgrade beds and ventilation, and to meet new safety codes (for example, sprinklers).

A not-for-profit independent and JCAHO-accredited institution, the hospital is operated and financially supported by a private corporation. The hospital employs a house staff of approximately 200 full- and part-time nurses and 35 physicians. Its remote location makes it difficult and expensive to recruit licensed

---

Security Act of 2002, the National Pharmaceutical Stockpile became the Strategic National Stockpile under the joint control of the Department of Health and Human Services and the Department of Homeland Security. The Strategic National Stockpile is a repository of antibiotics, chemical antidotes, antitoxins, life-support medications, IV administration, airway maintenance supplies, and medical and surgical items designed to supplement and resupply state and local public health agencies in the event of a national emergency anywhere and at anytime within the United States or its territories.

health care professionals. The hospital provides a wide range of specialty services, including cardiology, nephrology, obstetrics and gynecology, orthopedics, pediatrics and women's health. The hospital uses the local airport as its helipad and is designated a level-four trauma center.[4] It operates its own ambulance service. Two emergency department physicians are on staff.

The hospital is proximate to a military installation that closed its base hospital several years ago. In-patient military medical care is provided at Hospital Two, where military physicians have full privileges. Hospital ambulance services support the base as well.

Members of the hospital's administrative team describe being "more aware of the potential [for acts of bioterrorism and disease outbreaks] but not necessarily more prepared." They specifically cited the experiences of Toronto hospitals during the 2003 SARS epidemic as a sobering reminder of the vulnerabilities of hospitals to infectious disease outbreaks. "I don't know if there is enough of anything [human or other resources] to handle bioterrorism," one meeting participant noted. Hospital staff identified their specific vulnerabilities as including remote location, agricultural center, 10 minutes' walking distance to a border, proximity to a military installation, and the major trucking and rail lines that cross through the city, transporting millions of tons of freight annually.

Despite a significant investment in the purchase and installation of security cameras, only one security guard is on duty at all times. It was acknowledged that this guard is unable to monitor the cameras, patrol the 16 unlocked doorways and multiple other entrances in and out of the hospital, and respond to requests for assistance. Visitors have full access to the hospital without badging at or routing through a central entrance. Hospital staff indicated that a "suspicious" individual would be stopped, and recently an unfamiliar panel truck parked next to the hospital caused immediate concern. However, as one meeting participant noted, "The hospital is very diverse. We just think everyone is the relative of a patient." Janitors and maintenance staff might be able to backfill security during an emergency, but they have received no training. The hospital would look to the sheriff's office and the Border Patrol—both of which participate in preparedness planning efforts—to augment security functions in the event of a large-scale emergency.

The hospital's communications system is supported by a limited number of T1 lines[5] and an "antiquated" 911 system. "When we send ambulances to certain areas they are on their own because we can't communicate with them," one hospital representative noted. Another recalled a recent situation when a medevac helicopter could not be contacted for 45 minutes, and then only through a convoluted series of telephone chain calls. Although the Border Patrol is an important source of security backup, there is "no way to talk to them." Various community responder sectors are purchasing communications equipment, but participants were concerned that "some [devices] are analog and some are digital." Significant mention was made of the need for a communications infrastructure supported by repeaters and switches. The CDC's Health Alert Network is being developed, and satellite phones are a planned purchase.

---

[4] Trauma center designation levels set specific criteria and standards for determining the level of care a trauma victim needs and whether a particular hospital should treat the patient or transfer the patient to a trauma center that can administer more definitive care. Level-four trauma centers, the least capable on a scale from one to four, provide initial evaluation and assessment of injured patients. Most patients will require transfer to facilities with more resources dedicated to providing optimal care. Level-four trauma centers must have transfer agreements in place with more capable facilities.

[5] A T1 line consists of 24 individual channels, each of which supports 64k bits per second. Each channel can be configured to carry voice or data traffic.

The hospital feels it would be overwhelmed "in minutes" by more than 30 patients, probably far fewer if the emergency involved a communicable disease. The hospital is the "go to" place: "During a mass infection or disease outbreak people will want to come to your doors," noted one hospital employee. However, the hospital has only two negative-pressure isolation rooms, which would fill up quickly. The hospital has five ambulances, one of which is old: all ambulances cannot be kept locked and secured. Hospital Two has a memorandum of understanding to share resources with 23 regionally located hospitals over a 22-county area. A plan has been developed within the city and county to shut down the nearby international border if necessary. None of these plans has been tested through a drill or tabletop exercise, but the regional responders have conducted one drill testing their response to a chemical spill.

There is a five-day supply of food and three emergency generators that could run for 72 hours. Alerting the community during an emergency was reported as a serious problem. The literacy levels are low, and less than 10 percent of the population uses the Internet. Most people have phones, and the use of police bullhorns was mentioned as a possible alerting strategy.

The hospital's administrative staff also raised concerns about how they would be alerted to a threat, describing a situation in which there are no formal channels of information or specific guidance to hospital officials. "Every time [the Federal government] changes the threat level we don't know how or what to do differently," stated a hospital employee. "The EMS person might hear about a threat but he knows only because a higher-level EMS person mentioned it," stated one of the meeting participants. "We might get some bulletins from the state public health agency," noted another participant, "but that is usually after the fact."

Many obstacles to "preparedness"—a level that hospital leadership calculated was at a "two" on a scale of one to ten (ten being the most prepared)—were articulated. "The thinking part is easy, but the resources are difficult," stated the hospital COO. In addition to money, hospital preparedness will require significantly more and ongoing staff training, exercises, community education, and technical assistance. A portable tent in which to triage patients was cited as essential to mitigate the spread into the hospital of an infectious agent that could expose patients and staff. The hospital expressed a need for more trained professionals, especially nurses. There are no extra staff or nurse banks. School nurses might be able to provide assistance to the hospital, but this possibility has never been discussed with them. Additionally, as one participant noted, "In the event of a bioattack or disease outbreak everyone would want to respond, but we don't have enough protective equipment for them." Hospital volunteers are mostly senior citizens and would provide little staff backup during an emergency. Area nursing homes are filled to capacity and could not service an overflow of patients. "The city could open a facility," noted the mayor, "but how could it be manned?" Acknowledging limited capabilities for and training in biological agents, the hospital would look to the expertise and hands-on support from the nearby military base.

Hospital Three Profile

Hospital Three serves a population that is 85 percent African American and 97 percent English speaking. The average household income is $22,000; 33 percent of the county's residents are below the federal poverty level. Hospital Three is located in an agricultural area transected by an expanding major highway designed to support an increased volume of truck and tourist traffic. A port also exposes the area to shipping and barge traffic. The community is proximate to a nuclear facility.

Hospital Three is a 32-bed acute-care county hospital with both behavioral and chemical dependency units. The half-century-old facility, which receives only $200,000 annually in county funds, is severely dilapidated and in need of external and internal renovations, repairs, and modernization. A tour reveals mottled ceilings, wall and floor surfaces in dire need of paint, plaster and refurbishing, and spare and often makeshift patient facilities. An old and unreliable generator is available to provide limited power backup. In stark contrast to the poverty of the facility one notes the surplus of dedication exuded by the hospital staff, most of whom reside within the community this hospital serves.

The hospital employs 25 full- and part-time nurses and offers several outpatient services such as radiology, EKG, and ultrasound. "We don't offer [the community] a whole lot but what we offer they need," one participant noted.

Participants from Hospital Three expressed many concerns about terrorism and their lack of preparedness. When posed the hypothetical situation of a possible case of smallpox, one individual noted, "People would be exposed before we knew what was going on."

"A communicable disease would be tough to handle and tough to contain," another participant stated. There are no formal isolation procedures or supplies in place. The hospital has one (makeshift) negative pressure room, but staff has not been trained in true isolation procedures.

Surge capacity is extremely limited at this facility, which has no more than one day's worth of extra patient care supplies. There are no lists of trained personnel in or near the hospital's surrounding community, or retired staff that might be available to augment the limited number of hospital staff. A nearby nursing home is full and could not provide extra capacity for non-acute hospital patients who might have to be quickly moved from their acute-care hospital setting. The local elementary school has one licensed practical nurse to serve 1,000 pupils. The area's Federally Qualified Health Center[6] and the three to four local home health agencies that might have homemakers and aides who could provide assistance to the hospital during a large-scale event have not been involved in any bioevent or disaster planning. A subsidized private ambulance service, which staffs only one of its two ambulances at a given time, covers this hospital and hospitals in many other nearby counties. The hospital has no security staff to monitor and protect its nine entrances. Security support from the Highway Patrol reportedly would require "hours to respond."

The list of needs identified for expanding the hospital's preparedness capacities is extensive. The hospital's ventilation system is described as "primitive." Required supplies would include a spectrum of the basics: antibiotics, gloves, paper towels, and N95 masks.[7] Extensive training in biological agents and threats is a critical need. The few drills that have taken place have involved scenarios such as school shootings; none have addressed biological threats. Some training is available, but there is no one to cover jobs while individuals are absent.

---

[6] Federally Qualified Health Centers are health care organizations designated by Medicare legislation in 1991 to receive grant funding to provide care to underserved populations under Section 330 of the Public Health Service Act. Types of organizations that may receive 330 grants include Community Health Centers, Migrant Health Centers, Health Care for the Homeless Programs, and Public Housing Primary Care Programs (Centers for Medicaid and Medicare Services, Department of Health and Human Services, "Federally Qualified Health Centers"; http://www.cms.hhs.gov/providers/fqhc/. Also see Rural Assistance Center, "FQHC Frequently Asked Questions"; http://www.raconline.org/info_guides/clinics/fqhcfaq.php#whatis.

[7] N95 masks are lightweight, disposable masks designed to block particulate matter. "N95" is an efficiency rating from the U.S. National Institute of Occupational Safety and Health; it means that an N95 mask blocks about 95 percent of particles that are 0.3 micron in diameter or larger.

The hospital contains a few outdated personal computers supported by dial-up Internet access, but for the most part, communication equipment is old and lacks interoperability across responder sectors. One participant noted, "We can't talk with each other. The road manager can't talk to the Director of Civil Defense. [We need to be able to reach] the [emergency operations center], the sheriff and the county administrator.... Someone needs to work a radio to coordinate a response."

In the event of a biological attack or a mass-casualty situation, the hospital and the community anticipate assistance from the state health department. The state is in the process of writing and formulating response plans but is experiencing "the greatest shortage of nurses in its history." Multiple, simultaneous events would severely tax state resources and thereby limit the timeliness and number of deployable personnel to this and other hospitals.

Hospital Four Profile

Hospital Four is the only source of health care for an hour's drive in any direction. It serves a population of over 7,000 that is 75 percent Caucasian and 18 percent Native American. Local industry includes mining, lumber, and agriculture. The hospital is located a short drive from an international border, which is routinely and regularly traversed by local residents for recreation, sports, and dining.

Hospital Four moved to its present location in 1974. The facility contains 25 beds, of which 14 are used for long-term care. Both long-term and acute-care beds occupy the same wing of the hospital building and receive care from a shared nursing staff. Nurses cover these units as well as the emergency department. The emergency department in Hospital Four is telemedicine capable, but there are no ventilators or "specialized equipment" anywhere in the hospital. There is one room that is "designated," but not "approved," as a true negative-pressure isolation facility.

Without immediate transportation of seriously ill patients, "survivability would be low," noted one of the participants. However, winter fog routinely prevents helicopter transport, and airplanes can land only during daylight. During winter months, cold temperatures would prohibit appropriate pre-hospital triage of potentially communicable patients. The hospital has one 32-year-old generator that does not cover the entire hospital's non-emergency power needs. "A loss of emergency power [during winter months] would require complete evacuation of the hospital within one hour," noted a hospital official.

Members of the hospital's staff have begun to develop new policies to address the threat of bioterrorism. They participated in a state-sponsored bioterrorism tabletop exercise and realized the complexity of issues such as isolation, exposure screening, incident command, and adequate telecommunications (broadband Internet availability and cell phone service area) outside the township. The hospital is part of a regional response plan that includes 19 hospitals.

Staff of all levels of skills and expertise is at a premium in this community where "everyone wears multiple hats." Hospital officials are beginning to assemble lists of emergency personnel and phone numbers. Training is considered a critical need in all areas of preparedness, including triage, decontamination, bioagents, and disease management and detection. However, it is difficult to release staff for training, as there are no positions to backfill absent personnel slots. None of the hospital's staff received smallpox vaccinations during the Phase I vaccination program because the vaccinations were administered at only one state site, three hours away. Decontamination equipment and protective suits for law enforcement personnel are an expected state purchase in 2005. But, as one participant noted,

"Throwing equipment at us doesn't matter if you don't have people. We could have lots of decontamination [equipment] but who would handle it?"

Hospital Four is accessible through six entrances, all of which could be manually locked during an emergency. The master lock has not been changed since 1974 and there are reportedly "a lot of keys out there." But, as a hospital official noted, "Open doors are important in a small community for a hospital." The hospital does not have 24-hour security. All doors to treatment rooms, medical storage, files and sensitive equipment are key or keypad locked.

Community alerts from the hospital have, in the past, included use of a cable TV station, postings on local public buildings, and the use of educational videos in pizza parlors. In an emergency, however, the most effective strategy for getting the word out to this close-knit community is, as one participant noted, "to just tell two people."

Limited communication systems were noted repeatedly as a serious problem. "There are lots of dead spots because of the mountains," noted one participant.

"Cell phones are good for less than 10 percent of the time I drive and work," noted another participant.

"Hospitals can't talk with each other," a third individual reported.

As one participant described it, "The government is throwing equipment at us (the Sheriff's department finally received two more repeaters) but it's not compatible with the other equipment and the government is not funding installation or operation." The Sheriff's department also received handheld radios, which have not been programmed and for which no training has been provided. "The equipment came and that was that," noted one participant. Communication strategies, as well as improved technology, were noted as another important requirement. One participant noted that the emergency operations center gets overrun in the first hour of an incident such as a fire and comes to a standstill because of the huge influx of calls and use of multiple frequencies.

In the event that mass vaccination would be required, the hospital anticipates that state public health resources would be deployed to provide the bulk of expertise and hands-on administration "within five hours notice."

Hospital Five Profile

Hospital Five serves a population of 30,000 people, 92 percent of whom are native English speakers. The median household income is $35,000. Hospital Five is a short distance from an international border described by one participant as a conduit for "smuggling drugs, cigarettes, booze and people." At certain periods of the year the number of tourists exceeds by four times the number of indigenous residents.

Hospital Five is a JCAHO-accredited 49-bed hospital built in 1972. It provides a wide array of inpatient and outpatient specialty services supported by 75 registered nurse and 10 licensed practical nurse full-time equivalents. The filled-bed census averages 19 patients. The hospital has entered a service delivery agreement with a medical school that will make more specialized services available. The emergency room is staffed by full-time physicians and specialized nurses who are trained in many aspects of acute medical care. Emergency department staff provide local educational programs, continuing medical education, and quality assurance and will offer support and training to pre-hospital providers.

Hospital Five has one negative-pressure room and could create a negative-pressure environment in the emergency room through the use of portable high-efficiency particulate air filters and ductwork that vents outside. The fire department has a fully equipped hazmat trailer and a portable decontamination unit. The hospital has a 5,000-square-foot parking lot, which it would designate as a triage area during warmer weather.

Hospital Five is a member of a 16-hospital compact overseen by the state hospital association to provide mutual aid for staff, equipment, and triage in the event of a bioterrorism attack or large-scale disaster. Collegiality and partnership are the rule, not the exception, across a community of industry, academia (state college), emergency responders, and the hospital and health care providers, all of which have engaged at some level of preparedness and response discussions since Y2K.

In recent years hospital staff and other participants indicated far greater awareness for the potential of a bio or chemical terror incident. A recent prank that threatened to compromise the community's water system prompted the hospital's digging of its own well with a 40-gallon-per-minute capacity. The hospital has an 80-hour capacity for power from its backup generator and onsite fuel. Following September 11, 2001, the hospital immediately began to consider the impact of airline shutdowns on the delivery of medical supplies and the resulting ramifications for the ongoing hospital functions. As one hospital official noted, in an emergency "there is no coordinated plan to bring in materiel." Having moved from a just-in-time inventory system, the hospital now has a 30-day cache of routine medical supplies.

Acquiring replacement staff was a problem identified when considering the potential for a mass-patient event. As one participant noted, "Everyone wears multiple hats." The use of retired and home health nurses has been considered a plausible strategy to augment hospital surge capacity, but these individuals have not been included on rosters, nor have they participated in drills. The state is writing plans, which include prescribing a role for the National Guard to provide protection for hospitals in the event of bioterrorism and a surge in demand for medical services, as well as to assist in distributing materials from the Strategic National Stockpile. The Border Patrol[8] has been considered an important component of any bioterrorism response, but agreements for its participation have not been formalized.

Several members of the hospital staff have volunteered to receive smallpox vaccinations. Of the three ambulance companies designated to transport smallpox patients, two do not require respiratory protection for their workers and none have vaccinated employees.

The hospital has participated in a SARS tabletop exercise. "Drills help, but you never know until it happens," one participant noted.

Another indicated that it is difficult to envision the concept of a "large scale" event and that certain response procedures will depend on the season in which it happens, inferring the important role of weather and environmental conditions, adding, "[We] don't have a plan to transport noncritical patients out [because] where would they go?"

The hospital has 18 entrances, most of which are locked after 6 PM. After 8 PM only the admitting entrance is open to the general public. There is no security staff: the hospital incorporates a "security

---

[8] Since March 2003, the Border Patrol has been integrated with employees from the Department of Agriculture, the Immigration and Naturalization Service, and the Customs Service to create Customs and Border Protection, an agency within the Department of Homeland Security.

presence" of untrained but alert employees. There are 34 security cameras that run tape and are reviewed in the event of a problem.

Communication systems and technologies were reported to be a critical concern. The hospital has discussed information-sharing and capacity-augmenting strategies with local governments across the nearby international border. Power grids are vulnerable to the weather, and phone communication is susceptible to the mountainous terrain. In some spots it is difficult to communicate with ambulances. There is an inadequate number of cell towers. One participant noted, "At three o'clock when the college gets out all the cell coverage is jammed." Emergency medical services, fire, and police radios were recently upgraded, but the lack of local repeaters prevents seamless regional radio access. Additionally, the strategies underlying cross-sector communication activities were noted to be problematic. In the words of one participant, "This talking with everybody is relatively new. [We] have to understand who talks when."

The hospital participants indicated numerous requirements for improving preparedness capacity and capabilities, such as a respiratory protection program that would include the purchase of more equipment (N95 as well as self-contained breathing apparatus), fit-testing, and training programs. The hospital needs an ongoing staff-training program to improve and maintain skills, assure compliance, and provide appropriate record keeping. Participants noted the importance of building uniform plans across all hospitals statewide to assure consistency of training and equipment, especially at a regional level. Hazmat and emergency medical services have provided incident command training for the hospital; however, participants indicated that it was difficult to integrate the hospital response. More drills and exercises—especially cross border—are considered essential. "The state is on a learning curve for bio-preparedness," as one participant noted.

Summary and Conclusions

Five rural hospitals were selected to participate in a study of bioterrorism preparedness. Senior hospital administrators, clinical and managerial staff, their community's elected leadership, and representatives from the law enforcement, public safety, and public health sectors participated in guided discussions over a period of two days at each site. Discussions focused on the challenges rural hospitals and their communities are encountering in efforts to address the potential threat of disease epidemics resulting from deliberately released—or naturally emerging—infectious pathogens. Although findings based upon this methodology were not intended to infer the circumstances and opinions of all the country's rural hospitals, the experiences and concerns shared by these five hospitals may contribute useful insights to national hospital preparedness efforts—both urban and rural.

Site visits were conducted in five geographic regions of the United States: Northeast, Southeast, Midwest, Northwest, and Southwest. Each hospital visited as part of this study was selected because of its proximity to one or more designated factors that may increase a community's vulnerability to terrorism and the spread of a deliberately deployed communicable disease. These factors included proximity to international borders and potential targets of terrorism, such as the agriculture and farming industry, as well as military installations and nuclear facilities, and accessibility by major trucking and rail and shipping transportation lines and waterways.

Despite the unique qualities and vast distances separating each of the participating hospitals, the information shared and issues reported through the discussions yielded strikingly similar concerns. All participants demonstrated a keen grasp of their hospital's vulnerabilities within the context of the current national threat environment. In recognizing their community's status as a potentially attractive target, some participants had considered the possibility of being within the epicenter of a focused attack. Others suggested the potential for infection and contamination through inadvertent patient "downloads" from other hospitals, or other non-direct yet compromising scenarios. All study participants recounted efforts to initiate new policies and pursue training opportunities to improve their response capacities, skills, and understanding of pathogens and threat agents. Most noted that some progress has been made, particularly in terms of heightening their sensitivity to unusual events and in acknowledging the steep learning curve ahead.

All hospital study participants attributed their limited pace in attaining specifically improved preparedness capacities to the fact that promised funding has not yet arrived. "Everyday I read about resources coming," the CEO of one of the larger participating hospitals noted. "[I] have not seen one dime. [We] have not had one training session. Where is that money going because none of it is coming here? It's going to the big cities…. We have filled out endless documents and lists of resources and requests for equipment." Other hospital administrators made similar comments suggesting that homeland security–related funding for hospitals has yet to reach "the local level."

The deliberate release of most Class A biological agents, or a naturally occurring outbreak of a disease such as SARS, will require timely, expert and sustained response to halt the chain of person-to-person transmission. Rural hospitals have minimal person-power, which necessitates that "everyone wears multiple hats." There are no large reserves of staff within hospitals or their communities—few of those interviewed during the site visits have been able to identify nurse pools and other sources of trained personnel within their area that could provide surge capacity. Most of the hospitals that participated in

27

this study have relatively limited emergency department personnel and experience handling large-scale mass-casualty events. Furthermore, efforts to train existing personnel in the skills needed to address new threats have been limited by both the direct costs of tuition and offsite travel and the indirect costs associated with temporarily relieving staff from critical nursing and other duties. Augmenting local hospital response capacity through collaborative hospital efforts across geographic regions has been acknowledged as an important strategy and goal for addressing the large demand for medical care during a biological event. Hospital consortia have begun to articulate and develop consensus-driven response strategies that might contribute to the implementation of regional systems of response. Currently, the deficiency of interoperable skills and integrated procedures would limit attaining the desired levels of immediate seamless and efficient operations in the event that hospital personnel are deployed from one hospital to another during an emergency.

The problem of limited person-power is not uniquely characteristic of the hospital sector. Study participants from conventional responder agencies—law enforcement, firefighting, and hazmat teams—acknowledged that their sparse workforce would constrain the timeliness and sustainability of their response to a biological incident. Although they, too, have engaged in efforts to improve preparedness through training, expanding skill sets, and augmenting stores of equipment, there are no large reserves of personnel to handle their own responsibilities over the duration of an attack let alone to divert staff to supplement and protect hospital resources. Furthermore, efforts intended to formalize compacts of mutual aid with neighboring towns—often practical for ordinary emergencies like multi-alarm fires—may be more difficult within the context of terrorism and the potential exposure to weapons of mass destruction or mass disruption.

Networking and planning have significantly increased across the hospital and traditional responder communities—the sheriff's office, the fire department—to address perceptions of possible threats of terrorism, especially bioterrorism. However, these collaborative efforts remain relatively embryonic, as they have lacked both the resources and the technical guidance to build the cross-sector linkages required to contravene or mitigate the potentially devastating and unremitting sequelae of a biological attack or large-scale disease outbreak. Beyond the need to identify sufficient "expandable" resources across a community or within a region is the daunting effort to integrate these diversely trained personnel into a coherently functioning unit. As one hospital CEO succinctly expressed it, "[There are] lots of different agencies and organizations but it is extremely difficult to understand how they all come together."

Although the threat of a terrorist attack on a nuclear facility has become a more prominent concern in the post-9/11 climate, many rural hospitals have co-existed with nearby nuclear power facilities for decades. Hospitals also are familiar with responding to chemical spills and other situations requiring hazmat capabilities. Across the spectrum of possible weapons of mass destruction or mass disruption, biological agents present the most difficult challenges to rural communities, hospitals, and responders. The requirements of early clinical detection, swift and effective disease containment, and protection of hospital personnel and patients are especially overwhelming in relatively close-knit rural communities where hospitals were "never built to be secure—just friendly." Respondents at each of the participating hospitals felt that they would lack the ability to detect a large-scale biological event until much too late, at which point they would not be able to adequately protect the hospital staff or patients from exposure and infection. Many rural hospitals operate within a health care environment that lacks adequate negative-pressure isolation capabilities, patient cohorting strategies, and dedicated security personnel. The rural hospitals and pre-hospital providers, including EMTs, who participated in this study spoke of their limited access to both the training required to understand biological agents and personal protective equipment

(PPE). "[We] can wear the same turnout gear for years. But what about bio? Who's going to pay for the PPE?" asked one fire department official.

Most participants have recognized the importance of responding to a large-scale event within the rubric of well-defined leadership, expert skill sets, and practiced incident command. Unfortunately, many pre-existing response strategies still call for non-medically trained personnel, like law enforcement, to assume the lead within the community during a biological event—a situation that necessitates early and proficient medical expertise.

Most hospitals and their community partners recognize that "outside assistance" will be critical in the event of bioterrorism or a mass-casualty situation. Some hospitals operate under the belief that rapid and expert assistance could be expected from a nearby military facility or a state public health department. Yet conflicting priorities, untested response paradigms, and the potential for multiple, simultaneous demands for this expertise could well leave the hospitals precariously to their own limited resources. One local government official noted, "[I] have no more resources than I have had for years…. We have to have backup. Where will that come from? I can't call the National Guard because they're in Iraq. I can't depend on the Highway Patrol—it takes them hours to get to a [car] wreck." Some of the hospitals that participated in this study have attempted to improve their self-sufficiency by increasing supplies of pharmaceuticals, food, fuel, and, in one instance, potable water. However, most hospital administrators recognize that the nature of a biological event would challenge the basic capabilities and capacities of the average rural hospital. One hospital CEO noted, "In a rural setting we have always believed we are on our own. But this—[responding to] bioterrorism—we can't do by ourselves."

If a biological agent is released or a naturally occurring disease breaks out, swift containment and control of infection transmission are critically dependent on the integrated efforts of the hospital and the pre-hospital and responder communities. Instances may arise in which diverting potentially infected and contagious patients from a hospital may ultimately avert contamination and therefore preserve acute medical care capabilities. This will require clear and consistent channels of communication between the hospital and pre-hospital providers (for example, EMTs) in the field. According to all study participants, the communication technologies now supporting rural communities are not commensurate with the responsibilities of the rural hospital in the event of bioterrorism, a non-deliberate disease epidemic, or any other mass-casualty situation. The often-cited inadequacies in rural communication capabilities are clearly the result of a wide range of problems, including limited range of transmission and cellular infrastructure; signal interference due to geography and terrain; lack of interoperability of communication equipment across local, state, and federal sectors within and outside the community; radio frequency saturation from simultaneous civilian and responder use during peak demand periods; and incompatibility of multiple hardware platforms (repeaters, switches). One county official noted, "I have a cell phone in my pocket but I can't talk with my office one mile away."

Additionally, communication strategies between the hospital and the community are critical to protecting the limited resources of the rural hospital. Most participants spoke of their inability to alert the community to a health hazard and to meter the flow of people who require the administration of pre- or post-exposure vaccines or other medical countermeasures. One hospital CEO noted, "If you bring disease and panic into a small community we can spread it widely in a matter of hours. There is a lack of communication and education strategies to keep people safe and contained until appropriate equipment and personnel are brought in." Indeed, the very strength of the rural hospital—its friendly, open-door policy and designation as the "go to" place for medical care—is simultaneously its Achilles' heel. Multiple unlocked entrances make the inadvertent or deliberate introduction of infections into a hospital all too easy. The camaraderie and familiarity of hospital staff and patients often prevents incorporating within medical practices the most rigorous and immediate of disease control methods (personal protective equipment, pre-hospital triage for respiratory symptoms, etc.).

The plight of the rural hospital has not gone unnoticed by the public health sector. The role of the medical care delivery system is integral to the public health sector's mission of protecting populations and applying epidemiologic skills to characterize and monitor disease outbreaks. With that in mind, state public health department efforts, supported by federal CDC and Health Resources and Services Administration funds, are engaged in building preparedness plans that address the rural community. But on multiple occasions this study demonstrated that much of this planning is still in the development phase and that many of the existing disconnects between medicine and public health emerged as barriers to preparedness. Furthermore, several of the site visits and meetings in which rural hospital and state public health officials participated revealed that state preparedness planning has not been transparent to the rural communities. In some instances there has been no direct participation by the local medical and responder communities, and in other instances local officials were unaware of the scope of preparedness planning taking place at the state level.

America's rural communities are frequently a portal to its larger, more populated and urban areas. One hospital CEO's comment summarized the precarious state of affairs of the rural hospital in the current climate of threats: "We are as vulnerable and as important to the safety of the nation, but we don't have the financial wherewithal to protect the big cities if the entry point is here."

Recommendations

Since the attacks of 9/11 on the World Trade Center and the Pentagon and the subsequent anthrax attacks of 2001, America's collective psyche has suffered from the looming threats of terrorism and weapons of mass destruction or mass disruption, including the potential for the deliberate release of biological agents in civilian populations. Recent epidemics—and more recent re-occurrences—of SARS have been a reminder of the lethal and global effects of naturally occurring microbial pathogens.

Not the least of the United States' unprecedented actions to protect the homeland have been efforts to improve the capabilities of hospitals and their clinical personnel to detect, monitor, treat, and contain disease outbreaks. Residing in communities until recently perceived by policy makers and the public to be isolated and of little political value as targets of terrorism, America's rural hospitals face this challenge with limited specialized clinical personnel and inadequate isolation facilities, personal protective equipment, and systems of communication to coordinate and integrate their actions with the external responder community. Rural America's vital role in supporting our nation's critical infrastructure, including agriculture, food production, and the national highway system, disproves the pastoral notion of safety through seclusion.

Although this report focused on the capabilities of rural hospitals to function under exacting conditions such as a mass-casualty event, an infectious disease epidemic or an act of bioterrorism, it illuminates the critical importance of a national homeland security framework that integrates all components of the response community to assure the health, safety, and protection of its citizens and civil infrastructure. Aware of both the threat environment and the factors that increase their vulnerabilities, the hospitals that participated in this study have revealed critical areas of deficiency and systemic fragmentation in preparedness efforts across communities, regions, and states—deficiencies that must be addressed within America's resolve to protect both the nation's citizens and its economy. The following five recommendations may be the most initially compelling that require full and focused attention in the near term.

Develop a national consensus regarding the role of America's rural hospitals in bioterrorism preparedness.

The recognition of the new threat environment has widened the lens and the responsibilities of rural hospitals. All hospital study participants acknowledged that rural hospitals are likely to play a future role in detecting or responding to a bioterrorist attack or an infectious disease epidemic involving a novel pathogen. Unfortunately, in many of these hospitals the relatively limited capacity, facilities, and infrastructure (for example, security systems, communication systems, and heating, ventilation, and air-conditioning systems) are not designed to impede the spread of highly virulent or deliberately deployed infectious pathogens throughout the community and perhaps beyond.

Rural hospitals play a critical primary care role for the communities they serve. Preparing for and responding to bioterrorism is a new responsibility and, to a large extent, remains an unfunded mandate. Indeed, just as the critical role of hospitals in bioterrorism preparedness is being articulated, and rural vulnerabilities to terrorism are being recognized—at even the highest levels of government with Homeland Security Presidential Directive 9—the President's Budget request for 2005 reflects a significant cut to hospital preparedness funding nationwide.

It is vital to the national homeland security strategy that we articulate the contributions rural hospitals may offer in the response to a biological event and the demands that may be placed upon them if rural communities are directly targeted or indirectly affected. Preparedness strategies must emerge from a national dialogue and consensus among community leaders and experts in healthcare, defense, and other relevant sectors regarding the critical vulnerabilities and role of the rural hospital. A defined role and a nationally consistent, fully articulated construct for "minimal preparedness" capacity will guide efforts to train and equip rural hospitals for mass-casualty biological events. Resources must be directed toward achieving specific preparedness goals that will allow rural hospitals to make realistic and designated response contributions. Achievement of these goals should yield dual benefits, promoting the everyday business of rural hospitals as much as possible. Ideally, investments should improve rural health care while building preparedness.

Recommendation One: Action Items

The American Hospital Association and the Health Resources and Services Administration should convene a working group to facilitate national dialog regarding preparedness strategies for hospitals. The working group should consist of 15 to 20 organizations from the governmental and private sectors who are all key stakeholders in assuring that the country's medical infrastructure can withstand the demands of naturally occurring outbreaks of infectious disease and deliberate biological attacks. Such organizations should include JCAHO, the Secretary's Council on Public Health Preparedness, the CDC, the Agency for Healthcare Research and Quality, Business Executives for National Security, and the Department of Homeland Security, particularly agencies within that department engaged in border security and health activities. The deliverables of this working group should focus specifically on producing the following:

1. A comprehensive response checklist of steps to be taken by health care facilities in the first hours of a mass-casualty emergency. This checklist should be scalable consistent with hospital size and available resources (for example, for rural and small urban hospitals).

2. Measurable and self-assessable benchmarks for minimum hospital preparedness capabilities and capacities.

2

Validate expectations of external assistance in the event of bioterrorism or a large-scale epidemic.

Participants generally concluded that none of the hospitals was adequately designed, equipped, or prepared to respond to and control outbreaks of a highly communicable and potentially fatal infectious disease, especially if the disease were deliberately deployed. Representatives at each of the hospitals acknowledged that outside expertise and extra person-power would be required to augment the hospital's responsibilities in disease control and containment. They also noted their expectations that communicable patients would be expeditiously transported offsite to a specialized and tertiary care facility, leaving a stable and otherwise functioning rural hospital behind to handle the routine provision of medical services.

An exploration of the realities and capabilities of rural hospitals through the lens of this study demonstrated that many rural hospitals are not easily accessible—especially, for some, during the winter months. The rapid insertion of expertise may well be hampered for a variety of logistical and other factors. Conversely, transport from a rural hospital to a tertiary care facility may contribute to the survival ability of the index case and other acutely ill patients, but it will not necessarily relieve or ameliorate the ongoing burden of the rural hospital in its attempts to evaluate patients and implement medical countermeasures for others who may have been exposed. Indeed, the transport of contagious patients from the rural hospital may not be swift, permitting ongoing disease exposure to patients and staff within an environment of limited negative-pressure isolation facilities and personal protective equipment.

Participants at each hospital listed responder groups who they believed would assist them in the case of a health emergency, including the state public health department, the military, the sheriff's office, and the Border Patrol. Further discussions with representatives of these groups, however, revealed that while attempts would be made to provide some level of assistance, their primary responsibilities would restrict their ability to assure hospitals of their support.

Many of the discussions revealed that the hospitals' expectations of the source, scope, and timing of any external assistance are generally untested and, in some cases, unrealistic. For example, state public health departments acknowledged that their limited staffing, as well as the potential for multiple demands for assistance in the event of simultaneous outbreaks or attacks, would severely reduce their capacity to provide hands-on relief to rural hospitals. Furthermore, state public health departments are on a steep learning curve, refining their knowledge base and the operational skills necessary to address bioterrorism. Nearby military installations may be a repository of expertise, but in the event of an attack their primary mission and responsibilities will be warfighting.

Communities must engage in discussions to formalize agreements of assistance, roles, and responsibilities that are realistic and operational in the event of bioterrorism or mass casualties. Additionally, these relationships must be practiced through drills and simulations to ensure that diverse response sectors can work within an incident command structure.

Recommendation Two: Action Items

Engage the five rural hospitals that participated in this study in a series of preparedness exercises, including tabletops and full-scale community-based drills, to understand and delineate the roles and responsibilities of the hospitals and community and federal response partners from whom realistic expectations of assistance can be promised. Exercise participants should include, as appropriate and relevant, local border agencies (particularly those engaged in health activities), military installations, nuclear or chemical plants, and the business sector. These tabletops and drills will provide documented lessons learned as models that can be replicated to guide health care systems and hospitals, both urban and rural, across the country as they engage in building more robust preparedness efforts. The exercises and subsequent production of lessons-learned reports should be supported by private and federal stakeholders, possibly including the American Hospital Association, the Office of the Assistant Secretary for Public Health Emergency Preparedness, the Health Resources and Services Administration, the CDC Office of Emergency Preparedness and Response, the U.S.-Mexico Border Health Commission, and agencies within the Department of Homeland Security engaged in protecting the border and critical infrastructure.

3

Engage all sectors in integrating community-based planning and response efforts.

An outbreak of a contagious disease will impact the local community before spreading to distant locales. Many preparedness experts have acknowledged that the local community will be on its own for the first hours, if not days, of an attack or a serious disease outbreak. The quality of response during this initial time can make the difference between mitigating the spread of disease and allowing the progression of a far-reaching epidemic.

Despite the oft-noted axiom "All response is local," efforts at building local or regional capabilities remain disjointed at best. Most streams of preparedness funding are sector-specific (for example, specific streams of funds to police departments, fire and emergency medical services, public health, and hospitals) rather than community-centric. This "strategy" fails to give incentives for coordination, dilutes opportunities to merge expertise, and impairs efforts to capitalize on the gains in resource elasticity accruable from increased person-power and equipment. Moreover, current "sector-specific" preparedness planning and activities have resulted in few interoperabilities of human and technical resources, rendering the job of supplementing hospitals and communities during a time of crisis problematic.

Perhaps the most glaring and pervasive fault line articulated by study participants is the persistent lack of integration in preparedness efforts across all response sectors—including various levels of government, police and sheriff, emergency medical services and safety, public health. All respondents indicated strong commitments to their terrorism preparedness activities, but they also recognized the necessity of a cohesive, cross-sector, systemic response to effectively and efficiently parse out limited human and technical resources.

It is critical that we connect the funding and planning efforts *across* communities rather than in vertical, silo-like approaches within each sector. Such strategies will enable communities to integrate resources effectively and to build interoperable and expandable human and technical capabilities. The benefits of multi-sector collaboration and integrated capabilities are huge but require a level of joint effort that has yet to transcend political and administrative hurdles within many communities—and further into contiguous geographical regions. Rather than using a top-down approach, preparedness planning should be conceptualized from the bottom—or local level—up, with regard to the population, vulnerabilities, and requirements and capabilities necessary to protect populations and restore civil structures in the event of deliberate destruction or disruption. Preparedness planning subsequently should be funded and sustained from the local level as well.

Recommendation Three: Action Items

The U.S. Department of Homeland Security and the U.S. Department of Health and Human Services should establish a coordinating body, using the Information Sharing and Analysis Center model, to bring together lead funding and planning agencies across response sectors. This Preparedness Information Sharing and Analysis Center should be tasked with coordinating preparedness efforts and funding at the community level and integrating the response efforts of the usual responders (emergency medical services, police, and firefighters) and the medical and public health responders (public health departments, hospitals, and other health service providers). This coordination should focus on efforts to minimize stovepiping, which limits efficient use of preparedness funding and prevents the coordinated response activities that are critical to mitigating the effects of and morbidity associated with a natural emergency or deliberate disaster.

Expand training and improve the understanding of biological threats.

Responses to questions posed during study discussions reveal the disturbing pattern that biological threats remain the most poorly understood from across the range of potential disasters and weapons of mass destruction or mass disruption. Biological attacks develop in fundamentally different ways from incidents involving chemicals, radiation, or explosives—they can occur covertly; emergent and acute clinical settings may be the first lines of detection and response; and they are capable of spreading throughout populations until contained. These events, therefore, require public health and medical expertise and strong leadership with the authorities to requisition, direct, and commandeer appropriate and available resources. As such, more robust and continually refreshed education and training in biological disease events must be made available to the health care delivery sectors and their community responder colleagues.

Participants unanimously agreed that the lack of an adequate model for local bioterrorism preparedness training is a significant shortfall. Indeed, many study participants noted that acquiring such training remains one of the most pressing preparedness challenges facing rural communities, particularly due to cost and their inability to leave their job responsibilities during the work day.

Because funding and severely limited personnel backup systems restrict the use of offsite educational venues, it is incumbent upon federal agencies to develop community-based preparedness training modules that can be locally inserted. Additionally, by exploiting the dual-benefit, bidirectional capabilities of telemedicine systems (several of the rural hospitals that participated in this study have these systems in place for conference downlinking and physician oversight of nurse practitioners), distance education can be an additional and interactive vector for education and training.

Recommendation Four: Action Items

As a result of the products developed by the American Hospital Association and the Health Resources and Services Administration working group (see Recommendation One: Action Items), nationally applicable models for preparedness training and education should be developed. Leadership in this area could come from federally funded academic centers now involved in developing response curricula and training health care professionals with a particular focus on expanding capabilities and skills at a regional level to maximize human and technical resources. For example, the Colorado Biological, Nuclear, Incendiary, Chemical, and Explosives Training Center has initiated a statewide education program to train health care and public safety professionals in the fundamental principles of preparing for and responding to an event involving weapons of mass destruction. A similarly tasked academic center is the National Emergency Response and Rescue Training Center at Texas A&M University.

5

Install a reliable and interoperable rural communications platform.

The diversity and lack of interoperability among communication systems that are in place for many of our rural responders would restrict the effective integration of medical and non-medical personnel in responding to a bioterrorist attack or any other mass-casualty event. The Federal Communications Commission (FCC) and the National Telecommunications & Information Administration were directed by Congress as far back as the 1990s to work together to resolve incompatibilities among federal, state, and local public safety radio equipment and its spectrum usage. In response to this directive, the National Telecommunications & Information Administration issued a *mandate* to all federal agencies to shift their radio systems to what was then considered more spectrally efficient narrowband digital technologies (25 kHz) by 2008 (subsequent narrowband technologies have narrowed this bandwidth to as low as 6.25 kHz; movement to the lower bandwidth is still not uniformly approved). Correspondingly, the FCC in its Fifth Report and Order of July 2002 directed that new radio systems in the public safety band (700 MHz) would have to comply with the even more stringent 6.25 kHz channel bandwidth after December 31, 2006. However, since the FCC did *not mandate* that state and local responders move to the narrowband systems, but simply refused to approve new wideband frequency usage requests, the state and local responders, for economic reasons, were not required to change their existing systems.[1]

---

[1] Discussion with Frank E. Ferrante, President, FEF Group, LLC.

Throughout the 1990s, the communications industry has worked toward a solution to this problem. Recognizing the need for common standards for responders, representatives from the Association of Public Safety Communications Officials International, the National Association of State Telecommunications Directors, selected federal agencies, and the National Communications System established Project 25, a steering committee charged with selecting voluntary standards for interoperable digital public safety radio communications systems. Systems compliant with standards set by Project 25 have been increasingly adopted and deployed in responder communities.[2]

The existing patchwork of old and new radio systems (based on community funding available by locality) restricts community interoperation. Challenges faced by wireless systems in mountainous terrain and extreme weather require sophisticated redundancies and consideration of applying technologies that may not have previously been deployed locally (satellite telephones may be viable and should be considered as a backup offering when appropriate). To improve this situation, it is recommended that local, state, and federal responder communities be given a mandate to provide at least a minimal number of totally compatible systems and that funding sources be identified to assist in this procurement. State, local, and federal responder communities must focus more attention on building a real-time emergency communications system that fully meets needed interoperability conditions across medical, responder, and government sectors and vertically across levels of organization.[3] The Department of Homeland Security, with input from the states, must coordinate and mandate a minimal set of responder communications standards and guidelines. Present-day threats and vulnerabilities necessitate concerted efforts to solve the critical rural communications conundrums presented by systems interoperability and geographical isolation.

Recommendation Five: Action Items

The Department of Homeland Security should convene a working group of representatives from key information and communication technology vendors. This group should be tasked to develop the guidelines and funding mechanisms that will assure the interoperability of communication systems across response sectors, localities, and regions. The Department of Homeland Security should provide critical leadership in involving representatives of private industry, especially information and communication technology vendors, to solve this foundational homeland security challenge.

---

[2] Telecommunications Industry Association Online, "Project 25 (P25): Standards for Public Safety Radio Communications"; http://www.tiaonline.org/standards/project_25/.

[3] Note the Universal Service Fund established by the Telecommunications Act of 1996 and overseen by the Federal Communications Commission, requiring telecommunications companies in the U.S. to pay a portion of their revenues from customers into a fund that can be accessed by not-for-profit rural heath care organizations to finance communication development.

Final Thoughts

Protecting the homeland from terrorism has become one of the greatest challenges faced by the United States. The threats that have emerged in recent years have forced American organizations in numerous sectors to restructure, take on new and difficult responsibilities, and reconsider their role in the community, the state, and the nation. While we have only begun to work toward meeting the new and unfamiliar threat environment, many steps have been taken toward building the required capabilities and improving preparedness.

With the threat of terrorism and the realities of emerging infectious pathogens, protecting civilians has become a key component of achieving national security. Our hospitals will be our front line of defense in providing the medical response to bioterrorist attacks and large-scale epidemics. This reality is especially poignant in rural America, which supports much of the nation's economic vitality and critical infrastructure, but where communities are made vulnerable in depending on isolated hospitals with limited capabilities and capacities. Older hospitals face newer threats for which they are not prepared. It is time to focus on the role of the rural hospital and to equip it, its workforce, and its community with the resources necessary to address 21st-century biological threats.

www.ingramcontent.com/pod-product-compliance
Lightning Source LLC
Chambersburg PA
CBHW080109010626
45794CB00015B/3341